CW01337776

Success Factors

THE RIGHT STUFF

Comes With a 7-DAY
INTEGRITY CHALLENGE

WES BERRY

Business
Quick
Reads
Series Volume 6

Also by Wes Berry

Motivational Leadership & Business Series
*Big Things Have Small Beginnings: The Motivation
and Mindset that Build a $750-Million Business
(Book 1)*
*Success Factors: Million-Dollar Concepts that Work
for Everyone (Book 2)*
*Master the Metaverse: Multi-Million Dollar Investment
Opportunities (Book 3)*

Business Quick Reads
The Positive Side of Golf: Motivation (Vol 1)
Ice Cream Therapy: Mindset (Vol 2)
Icons of Success: Leadership (Vol 3)
The Ritz Experience: Growth and Scalability (Vol 4)
Ty Cobb, Babe Ruth, and So On: Teamwork (Vol 5)
The Right Stuff: Integrity (Vol 6)
The Two Steves: Core Competencies (Vol 7)
FUD Moneyball: Change (Vol 8)
Get On Board: Inclusion (Vol 9)
Stress Is My Superpower (Vol 10)
Outcome Based Sales (Vol 11)
Effective Communication (Vol 12)

THE
RIGHT
STUFF
And 7-DAY INTEGRITY
CHALLENGE

By: Wes Berry

America's NASA Space Program in the 1960s was of necessity grounded in technical and physical integrity. And that integrity was tested by the events of January 27, 1967. Apollo 1 was running through a launch rehearsal at the NASA complex at Cape Kennedy. The mission was planned to launch on February 21, 1967 and would be the first flight of the Apollo Program, which would eventually land the first men on the Moon. Command Pilot Gus Grissom, Senior Pilot Ed White, and Pilot Roger B. Chaffee were selected to man the mission. These three men were considered the "Best of the Best" after some of the most intensive selection, conditioning, and training that mankind has ever devised. Yet on that day, the integrity of NASA failed.

It was a failure of engineering and of manufacturing, some poorly constructed electrical system resulting in a fire caused by a spark—a catalyst that ignited the high pressure, pure oxygen atmosphere of the cabin. With no means of escape designed into their space capsule—no emergency evacuation or fire suppression system—it became a death trap. And to top it off, nobody thought pressurized, pure oxygen was a risky idea.

On July 20, 1969, some 30 months after the Apollo 1 fire that took the life of all three of its crew members, a new chapter for mankind was being written. This time it was Apollo 11's turn, and Neil Armstrong, Michael Collins, and Buzz Aldrin traveled 238,900 miles to the Moon. Armstrong and Aldrin landed the lunar module Eagle. Armstrong's first words upon stepping on the surface were, "One small step for man, one giant leap for mankind." NASA had met the challenge, and in the process they restored their integrity.

It could be argued that without the Apollo 1 fire, NASA might never have made it to the Moon. Integrity is a very precious and perishable thing, and like a great love, it requires constant passion.

Jonas Salk, who created the original polio vaccine, was a man of integrity. Today, the creation of a widely-used vaccine like Salk's would be a cash cow for a pharmaceutical company. Their patents would likely generate significant income for many years to come.

However, Salk refused to patent his creation, passing up the opportunity to make millions of dollars. In his view, the vaccine belonged to everyone. When he was asked who owned the rights to the vaccine, he replied: "Well, the people, I would say. There is no patent. Could you patent the sun?" [1]

Now, I'm not here to make anyone feel ashamed about profiting off their work. Developing new medicines is expensive, time-consuming work, and much of the money these companies make gets poured into research for the next project.

Still, you have to admit that Salk's decision to not patent his vaccine and to instead give it to the people is remarkable, and it reveals one of the most important character traits that, sadly, isn't front and center for many businesses and individuals today.

That character trait? Integrity.

What Is Integrity?

Integrity is one of those words where everyone feels like they know what it means, but when they actually have to define it, it can be tough to put it into the right words. You know it has something to do with doing the right thing, something to do with trust, but for some reason, it's difficult to pin it down exactly.

I think a lot of this is because integrity is an idea. Before we can understand what we mean when we talk about integrity, we have to take a few minutes to unpack everything this dense, important word contains.

The best place to start unpacking is also the simplest: integrity means keeping your promises. When you act with integrity, it means that you've given someone your word that you'll do something and that you follow through on that promise. Just like the U.S. Postal Service, you always deliver on your word, come rain, or snow or gloom of night.

But delivering on your promise or keeping your word to yourself and others isn't just about a simple act of exchange. No, what it's really about is trust. Having integrity is about creating relationships built on trust, which means that people know they can rely on you to not only follow through on your word, but that you'll go out of your way to make sure you keep your promises, too.

Of course, this trust doesn't just happen on its own. It has to be built over time, with each kept promise building on the last, helping you to establish a reputation for trustworthiness. It's a lifetime process, building trust, and the more people come to rely on you, the higher the stakes are raised.

On the flip side, trust can be broken in a matter of seconds. One missed delivery, one small oversight, even a simple misstatement, can take years to repair. Sometimes, those rifts become permanent.

Not to sound too negative, but this is going to happen to you at some point. It's impossible to be perfect all the time, and sooner or later, there's going to be a slip-up, someone is going to be disappointed, and that trust is going to be shaken. The only way to keep a breach from wrecking your reputation is to continually strive to act with integrity in all aspects of your life.

This goes for both individuals and for businesses. For both, the concept of integrity is multi-dimensional and complex. It encompasses honesty, transparency, accountability, and ethical behavior. Integrity is a fundamental value that shapes the way individuals and organizations interact with each other. It is an essential trait that builds trust, credibility, and reputation, which are crucial for the success of any enterprise In today's world, where information is readily available, the importance of integrity has become more significant than ever. Thus, integrity is important for both individuals and enterprises, and has a significant impact it has on their performance and success.

Let's take a closer look at each of these separately.

The Importance of Integrity for Enterprises:

The importance of integrity for enterprises cannot be overstated. In today's highly competitive business environment, trust and credibility are critical for success. Customers, investors, and regulators expect enterprises to operate with integrity and transparency. Enterprises that fail to meet these expectations are at risk of losing customers, investors, and their reputation.

A recent study by EY found that 97% of investors consider ethical behavior to be a crucial factor when making investment decisions. The same study found that 59% of investors have divested from companies due to ethical concerns. These findings demonstrate that enterprises that operate with integrity have a significant competitive advantage over those that do not.

Integrity also plays a crucial role in attracting and retaining talent. Employees want to work for enterprises that share their values and exhibit ethical behavior. A recent survey by PwC found that 77% of millennials consider a company's purpose and values when deciding where to work. Enterprises that fail to uphold high standards of integrity are likely to struggle with attracting and retaining top talent.

Moreover, enterprises that operate with integrity are less likely to face legal and reputational risks. They are more likely to comply with laws and regulations, which reduces their exposure to legal risks. They are also less likely to face reputational risks, as they are perceived as trustworthy and reliable.

A Company Without Integrity

Enron Corporation was a multinational energy company based in Houston, Texas. Founded in 1985, Enron was one of the largest energy companies in the world, with annual revenues of $101 billion in 2000. However, in 2001, Enron filed for bankruptcy, and its senior leaders were charged with various crimes, including securities fraud, insider trading, and money laundering.

Enron's collapse was primarily due to its lack of integrity and ethical behavior. The company engaged in a range of fraudulent activities, including the manipulation of financial statements and the creation of off-balance-sheet entities to hide debt. Enron's senior executives, including CEO Kenneth Lay and CFO Andrew Fastow, were complicit in these activities and misled investors, regulators, and employees about the company's financial health.

Enron's lack of integrity had severe consequences for its stakeholders. Thousands of employees lost their jobs and their retirement savings. Investors lost billions of dollars, and Enron's collapse had a ripple effect throughout the energy industry.

16

Enron's case highlights the importance of integrity for enterprises. The company's lack of integrity led to its downfall and had severe consequences for its stakeholders. Enron's collapse also led to greater scrutiny of corporate governance and ethics, which resulted in the passing of the Sarbanes-Oxley Act of 2002. The Act established new standards for corporate governance and required greater transparency in financial reporting.

The Importance of Integrity for Individuals:

Integrity is also essential for individuals. Individuals who exhibit integrity in their personal and professional lives are more likely to be respected, trusted, and successful. They are perceived as trustworthy, reliable, and ethical, which enhances their reputation and credibility. They are also more likely to build strong

17

relationships with others, which can lead to new opportunities and collaborations.

Integrity also plays a crucial role in personal development. Individuals who exhibit integrity are more likely to have a strong sense of self and a clear moral compass. They are more likely to make decisions that align with their values and beliefs, which leads to a greater sense of fulfillment and satisfaction.

Moreover, individuals who exhibit integrity are more likely to be resilient in the face of challenges and setbacks. They are more likely to learn from their mistakes and use them as opportunities for growth and development.

A Fraudulent Man

Bernard Madoff was a former stockbroker and investment advisor who perpetrated one of the most significant financial frauds in history.

Madoff's investment firm, Bernard L. Madoff
Investment Securities LLC, was founded in 1960
and was highly respected in the financial industry.
However, in 2008, Madoff confessed to running a
Ponzi scheme that defrauded investors of over $65
billion.

Madoff's lack of integrity had severe
consequences for his investors. Many of them lost
their life savings, and the fraud had a ripple effect
throughout the financial industry. Madoff was
sentenced to 150 years in prison and became a
symbol of greed and corruption in the financial
industry.

Madoff's case highlights the importance of
integrity for individuals. Madoff's lack of integrity
not only had severe consequences for his investors
but also had a significant impact on his own life.
Madoff's lack of integrity led him to engage in

19

criminal behavior that ultimately destroyed his reputation and his life.

Integrity Is More Than a Character Trait

That's a key point. Integrity is action; it's about what you do more than what you say. It's true that talk is cheap. You can promise anything, but it's your

> *Your success is never final; for every day it must be won, yet failure is never permanent.*

ability to follow through that counts. Your word is your bond, but that means nothing if it's not accompanied by actions. But how do you decide which actions are right? How do you determine the right course of action at any given point?

The answer is to establish your own code of values and principles. Values are the deeply embedded ideas that reflect the beliefs and moral attitudes that guide your choices. Principles, on the other hand, are fundamental rules that govern how the world functions. While values tend to evolve over time, or shift as situations change, principles usually remain fixed.

Patience is a good example of a value. It's good to be patient when waiting for investments to pay off, but less so when a critical delivery is several hours late. On the other hand, principles are more universal. Take honesty. If you lie to someone, the only reliable outcome is that you become less trustworthy.

Your guiding values and principles stem from your own belief system, whether you're establishing them for yourself or for your company. You should be willing to consult with other sources, including people, books, articles, and anywhere else you turn to for guidance. But ultimately, your code is yours and yours alone, and it will ideally become the baseline guiding force in all of your decision-making.

Keanu Reeves is one of the most successful actors in American film history. From his early days as a stoner comedian in *Bill and Ted*, to action stardom in movies like *Speed*, *The Matrix*, and *John Wick*, Reeves is one the most recognized film stars in America. However, Reeves has never let his success—and the money that came with it—go to his head.

Instead, Reeves has stayed true to his own personal values and principles. On multiple occasions, he's taken less money in order to hire the actors he believed would make his movies more successful.

In *The Devil's Advocate*, Reeves insisted they bring Al Pacino on board, cutting millions from his salary in order to make it happen. The same thing happened when he brought Gene Hackman on board for *The Replacements*. He also turned down a lucrative contract for *Speed 2*, believing the sequel would be a pale imitation of the original. [2]

Reeves has also donated a significant portion of his earnings to a number of charities, including several children's hospitals. These donations have helped keep these hospitals running, providing badly needed care to communities. For his part, Reeves prefers to keep these donations quiet—he's more concerned with making sure people get the help they need than in receiving "credit."

Reeves is a great example of someone living a life of integrity. He's guided by his values and principles, even if it results in him making less money at times. He has established values and principles that provide a clear path forward, allowing him to feel comfortable with his choices.

While every person has to establish their own set of principles and values, there are a number of values that should be important to everyone. For instance, honesty and respect are two of the most important factors in living a life of integrity.

Consider the Golden Rule: do unto others as you would have them do unto you. When you treat people honestly, you inspire others to be honest with you. On the flip side, if you try to deceive others, you're much more likely to be deceived yourself. The same goes with respect. If you want others to respect you, you need to grant them the same courtesy.

Perhaps even more important is fairness. This is especially true as businesses focus more on issues of diversity and inclusion in the workplace.

Ensuring that all applicants receive an equal opportunity is a good first step. However, truly embracing diversity and inclusion goes far beyond hiring. Instead, it's about ensuring trust, not only among your workforce, but also within the business community.

Building Integrity

As I said before, integrity isn't something that just happens overnight. You'll never wake up one morning and think to yourself, "Hey, now I have integrity!" No, building integrity is an ongoing, lifelong process, one that you'll need to live every day.

Ideally, integrity will become a habit. Even then, you'll still need to be aware of how your actions reflect your integrity. Here are just a few ways you can build the integrity habit into your life.

25

Establish Your Values and Principles

You probably know this already by now, but I'll say it again: Knowing your values and principles is really important! Whether you're focusing on your business or yourself, establishing these basic guiding ideas is critical to making the right decisions at any given time. And these values and principles aren't just for you—they make up the core of the identity you present to the world.

Take Amazon, for example. Founder Jeff Bezos started Amazon in 1994 as an online bookstore operating out of his garage—often delivering packages himself. One year after their IPO in 1997, the company started expanding beyond books, and while they wouldn't turn a profit until 2003, they eventually became the retailing behemoth they are today.

A huge part of their success has been focusing on the customer experience. From their one-click checkout system to the sheer volume of goods, Amazon is focused on making online shopping as easy and customer-friendly as possible.

This is especially clear in their return policy. Shopping online is fundamentally different than going into a brick-and-mortar store, where you can physically inspect a product before you buy it. Amazon understands this, and they make returning items easy—and usually free for their Amazon Prime members.

Amazon allows customers to return almost anything within 30 days of purchase with no restocking fee. You can print and package the return yourself, or you can drop the item off in an Amazon locker or a partner store, like Whole Foods or Kohl's. Your refund is then automatically processed, making the process virtually painless. [3]

Amazon decided early on that the customer experience was central to their company's values, and they trusted the principle that satisfied customers turn into repeat customers. They embedded integrity into their business model— and you only need to look at the company's ledgers to see how well that's paid off.

Make—and Keep—Promises

Keeping your word is central to the idea of integrity, and the only way to prove that you're trustworthy is to demonstrate it. That means that you have to make promises to people, guarantees that you'll meet certain performance metrics, however you decide to determine them. But what really matters is that you follow through on those promises.

This is where the philosophy of under promising and overdelivering comes into play.

When you're making a commitment to someone, it's important not to overextend your ability to deliver. After all, it only takes one broken promise to damage your credibility. On the flip side, you need to be wary of making promises that are too small—don't completely undermine your abilities.

In essence, it's about finding a balance between stretching yourself to reach new heights without overestimating your abilities. Your integrity depends on finding that balance, and as long as you're true to yourself, then you should have no problem making that assessment.

Always Be Honest

If trust is the backbone of integrity, then honesty is the rest of the skeleton. In order for anyone to trust you, they need to believe that you're being honest with them throughout your entire interaction. Even a small fib, one that seems

29

harmless at the time, can come back and cause enormous problems down the road, potentially ruining your credibility.

Honesty starts with your initial promise. As I mentioned earlier, you need to make sure you set realistic but ambitious goals for what you can deliver. Then you need to be able to clearly communicate that promise to others, being sure that both sides understand exactly what is being promised, including deadlines and timelines.

In the event that something does happen, and you can't meet your commitment, you can preserve your integrity by being honest. Problems are inevitable in all walks of life, and most people will understand if someone makes a mistake.

Instead of trying to cover it up, own your mistake and do whatever it takes to resolve the situation. Sometimes, that honesty can be even more effective in building a relationship of trust.

Stay Mission-Focused

One of the best ways to develop your values and principles into a working format is to use them as part of your mission statement. That statement can then serve as a set of guiderails to help direct your actions.

Setting your company's mission in clear, unambiguous language helps you to establish an identity for your company. When your customers know what you stand for, they know what to expect from your company, not only in terms of products or services, but in how you do business.

If customers know that your business stands for something beyond profit, they're more likely to align themselves with your interests and that can have far-reaching benefits for you.

Surround Yourself with Integrity

There's an old saying: you can tell a lot about a person by the company they keep. When it comes to integrity, this is especially true. You should make every effort to surround yourself with

> *The more hands money passes through, the more fingers it can stick to.*

people who hold similar ideals to you, whose values and principles align with those held by you and your company.

Your environment matters, and whether you notice it or not, your behavior is influenced by those you spend time around. The more time you spend around someone who isn't trustworthy, the more tempting it may be to cut corners here and there or to fudge numbers in some accounts.

Instead, cut ties with those whose integrity is lacking, and spend more time with those whose influence will be a positive force in your life.

Conclusion

It's tempting to reduce integrity to "doing the right thing." But the problem, of course, is knowing exactly what "the right thing" is. There's no single, universal answer that applies to every person in every situation. But when you take the time to truly understand the values and the principles that you believe should guide your actions, then you've got a good shot at getting it right.

There are some values that are intrinsic to the idea of integrity. Honesty. Equality. Fairness. Diversity. Respect. Trust. These are all values that should guide your sense of integrity. No matter who you are or where you're from, when you treat others with integrity, more often than not, they'll return the favor.

In a recent article in the *Harvard Business Review*, it was found that enterprises with high integrity ratings have a higher return on assets and a lower cost of capital. The study also found that individuals who exhibit integrity have higher job satisfaction and better mental health outcomes.

You can see why it's essential for individuals and enterprises to prioritize integrity in their personal and professional lives. Upholding high standards of integrity is not only the right thing to do, but it is also essential for long-term success and sustainability.

ALMOST THE END! YOU STILL NEED TO COMPLETE THE 7-DAY CHALLENGE!

7-Day Integrity Challenge

Why Accept this Challenge?

If you're seeking personal growth and development, you need to commit to consistent effort. One way to jumpstart this journey is by taking the 7-Day Challenge. To succeed in this challenge, you must dedicate a little time each day to contemplation and reflection on the given topic.

The questions provided are only a starting point. If they don't resonate with your personal experiences, modify them to better suit your situation. This flexibility allows for a more meaningful and authentic exploration of the subject matter.

When you commit to this challenge, you're making a decision to actively engage with your thoughts and emotions. Writing down your reflections is a powerful tool to solidify your insights and gain clarity on your internal landscape. This daily practice can have a profound impact on your overall well-being.

Approach this 7-Day Challenge with an open mind and willingness to explore. You may uncover aspects of yourself that you weren't previously aware of or gain a deeper understanding of your values and priorities. This challenge's benefits extend beyond the initial 7 days, and the act of carving out time for introspection and self-reflection can become a habit.

Ultimately, this challenge is a powerful tool for anyone seeking to enhance their self-awareness and personal growth. By dedicating a small amount of time each day to contemplation and reflection, you are taking an important step towards a more fulfilling and meaningful life. Upon completion, commit to re-reading and updating this challenge when you find yourself challenged by this concept in the future.

A 7-day Challenge provides a roadmap for achieving your goals by breaking them down into smaller, achievable tasks. By having a clear challenge, you can stay motivated and focused on your goals. Each day's challenge builds upon the previous day's, creating momentum towards the desired outcome. Additionally, having a plan can help you stay organized and prioritize tasks based on their importance and urgency.

A challenge can help you overcome procrastination and stay accountable. By having a clear outline of what needs to be done, you can avoid feeling overwhelmed and take action towards your goals. Furthermore, having a plan can help you track your progress and make adjustments as needed.

Overall, a 7-day Challenge is a powerful tool to focus on a particular issue and provide greater insight, bringing an area of concern into your comfort zone.

Day 1: Define Your Values

The first step in achieving and maintaining integrity is to define your values. What is most important to you in life and work? What do you stand for? Once you have a clear understanding of your values, you can use them as a guide for decision-making and behavior.

For enterprises, it is crucial to define the company's values and communicate them to employees, customers, and stakeholders. When everyone is on the same page about what the company stands for, it is easier to uphold high standards of integrity.

NOTES:_____

_____

_____

_____

_____

Day 2: Be Honest and Transparent

Honesty and transparency are essential components of integrity. Be honest in your communication with others, even when it is difficult. If you make a mistake, own up to it and take responsibility. Be transparent in your actions, decisions, and communications. When you are open and honest, you build trust with others.

For enterprises, honesty and transparency are crucial for building trust with customers, investors, and regulators. Be open about your business practices, financial performance, and any potential risks or challenges.

NOTES:_____

_____

_____

_____

_____

Day 3: Uphold Ethics and Compliance Standards

Ethics and compliance are critical for maintaining integrity. Uphold high ethical standards in your personal and professional life. Follow laws and regulations and be proactive in identifying and addressing potential compliance risks.

For enterprises, it is essential to have a strong compliance program and a culture that values ethics and compliance. Train employees on ethical behavior and compliance standards and hold them accountable for upholding these standards.

NOTES:_____

_____

_____

_____

_____

_____

Day 4: Build Relationships Based on Trust

Integrity is closely tied to trust. Build relationships based on trust with others by following through on your commitments, being reliable and dependable, and treating others with respect and fairness.

For enterprises, building trust with customers and stakeholders is essential for long-term success. Focus on building positive relationships based on trust by delivering quality products and services, being responsive to customer needs, and being transparent in your business practices.

NOTES:_____

_____

_____

_____

_____

_____

Day 5: Lead by Example

As an individual or as a leader in an enterprise, lead by example when it comes to integrity. Set a positive example for others to follow by upholding high standards of ethical behavior, being honest and transparent, and building relationships based on trust.

For enterprises, leaders play a crucial role in upholding high standards of integrity. Set a positive example for employees by demonstrating integrity in your actions and decisions, and by holding others accountable for upholding ethical behavior and compliance standards.

NOTES:_____

_____

_____

_____

_____

_____

Day 6: Continuously Evaluate and Improve

Integrity is not a one-time event but a continuous process of evaluation and improvement. Continuously evaluate your personal and professional behavior to ensure that it aligns with your values and ethical standards. Identify areas for improvement and take action to address them.

For enterprises, continuously evaluate your business practices, compliance program, and culture to ensure that they align with your values and ethical standards. Identify areas for improvement and take action to address them to continuously uphold high standards of integrity.

NOTES:_____

_____

_____

_____

_____

_____

Day 7: Contemplation and Reflection

On the last day of the challenge, take some time for contemplation and reflection. Reflect on the past week and evaluate how well you upheld high standards of integrity. Consider the challenges and successes you experienced, and identify areas for improvement.

For enterprises, take some time for contemplation and reflection on your company's commitment to integrity. Reflect on your successes and challenges, and identify areas for improvement to continuously uphold high standards of integrity.

NOTES:_____

_____

_____

_____

_____

_____

_____

Conclusion

Achieving and maintaining the quality of integrity is a continuous process that requires commitment and effort. By defining your values, being honest and transparent, upholding ethics and compliance standards, building relationships based on trust, leading by example, and continuously evaluating and improving, you can uphold high standards of integrity both as an individual and as an enterprise.

References

1.   Tan, Siang Yong and Ponstein, Nate. "Jonas Salk (1914-1995): A Vaccine Against Polio." *Singapore Medical Journal* (Jan. 2019), Vol. 60.1. National Center for Biotechnology Information. https://www.ncbi.nlm.nih.gov/pmc/articles/PMC6351694/

2.   King, Tom. "Action Star Keanu Reeves Wants to Play the Field." *The Wall Street Journal* (7 September 2001). https://www.wsj.com/articles/SB99981402381538 4990

3.   Phillips, Ashley and Bufete, Tercius. "A Complete Guide to Amazon Prime's Return Policy." Business Insider (25 May 2021). https://www.businessinsider.com/amazon-prime-return-policy

5.   Jaquith, Andrew. "Everything was green. Mulally thought that was odd for a company losing billions." Markerbench (21 February 2013).

https://www.markerbench.com/blog/2013/02/21/
Mulally-leadership/

6.   Polonskaia, Alina and Royal, Mark. "How
the World's Most Admired Companies Drive
D&I." HR Executive (10 December 2019).
https://hrexecutive.com/how-the-worlds-most-
admired-companies-drive-diversity-and-
inclusion/

7.   Agovino, Theresa. "Companies Try a New
Approach to Diversity, Equity and Inclusion:
Honest Conversations." Society for Human
Resource Management (4 August 2020).
https://www.shrm.org/hr-today/news/hr-
news/pages/a-new-approach-to-diversity-equity-
and-inclusion.aspx

8.   Dingle, Derek T. "Two Years After
Landmark Racial Bias Training, Starbucks
Advances Civil Rights and Inclusion Agenda."
Black Enterprise (29 May 2020).
https://www.blackenterprise.com/two-years-after-
racial-incident-starbucks-advances-civil-rights-
and-inclusion-agenda/

About The Author

Wes Berry is a Keynote Speaker and Workshop Facilitator with the professional skills and real-life experience to deliver on any stage. He works with Fortune 500 companies like Johnson & Johnson to smaller businesses and associations of all sizes that are seeking a breakthrough experience. Wes changes lives and transforms organizations by delivering a Paradigm Shift. He has written sixteen business and success books and is a *Wall Street Journal* best-selling author and TEDx speaker. As an entrepreneur, he built a $750 million international company that operated in 130 countries.

His business knowledge and communications skills have made him an expert media contributor on many topics, from commercial drone applications to the downsizing of Sears, resulting in appearances with various media outlets. His many media appearances include NPR, *The Wall Street Journal*, *The London Times*, *Entrepreneur* and *Time* magazines, Fox News, Neil Cavuto, Geraldo Rivera, and John Stossel, to name just a few.

Visit his website at WesBerryGroup.com to learn more.

Printed in Great Britain
by Amazon